HISTORIC PARLIAMENTARY DOCUMENTS IN THE PALACE OF WESTMINSTER

SECOND EDITION

LONDON

HER MAJESTY'S STATIONERY OFFICE

1975

HISTORIC PARLIAMENTARY DOCUMENTS
IN THE PALACE OF WESTMINSTER

By MAURICE BOND, O.B.E., *Clerk of the Records in the House of Lords*

FEW visitors to Westminster, seeing the Victoria Tower rising proudly at the southern end of the Houses of Parliament, realise its function. It was built a century ago by Sir Charles Barry for the safe-keeping of the historic documents of Parliament, and it has continued to serve this purpose ever since. Today, some three million documents are stored within the Tower, above the Sovereign's Entrance. Near the foot of the Tower, in the main building, is the House of Lords Record Office, which has immediate care of the Tower, and to the Search Room of this office historians, lawyers and members of the public come daily to inspect the records of Parliament.

These are, in the main, records of the House of Lords, for, from the Middle Ages, the clerk who now serves the Upper House (the 'Clerk of the Parliaments') has had custody of records which belong to Parliament as a whole, such as the master-copies of Acts, as well as of the internal records of the House. Documents belonging to the House of Commons were for long kept by the Clerk of that House in separate custody, but, with the principal exception of the original Journals, they perished in a fire which burnt down nearly the whole of the Palace of Westminster in 1834. The Lords' documents survived because they were then kept in the more remote Jewel Tower, on the other side of Old Palace Yard.

By 1864, these records had been transferred from the Jewel Tower to the newly-built Victoria Tower, and there they survive today in the most varying types of format. Some are in book form, very many are on rolls of parchment, and an important section of modern records consists of plans and maps (see page 17). Amongst the more unusual records are large gravestones, brought into the Lords as evidence in a peerage claim, and a lengthy petition from East Africa, bearing many hundreds of thumb-marks to attest the names of the petitioners. The latest records include a great deal of photographic material, audio-tape and cine-film.

THE SIXTEENTH CENTURY

The earliest document preserved in the Victoria Tower dates from 1497. Before that time, the records of Parliament were transferred at the end of a session to Chancery, and are now preserved with other records of that department in the Public Record Office. The first documents surviving from 1497 are the original Acts of Parliament. Journals of the House of Lords are preserved from 1510. Papers laid on the Table of the Lords from 1531, and Journals of the House of Commons from 1547.

Plate 1 (page 5) shows a leaf from an early Lords' Journal, which records the passing of the first Act of Uniformity in 1549. It has an unusual and important note appended of the names of peers who voted against the bill (some 11 out of a total attendance of 52). In Plate 2 (page 6) may be seen a typical original Act, the Poor Law of 1601, which finally established the principle that the local community was responsible for the care of the poor. It was written on a vellum roll 13 inches wide and 7 feet long. (Some rolls of this type are as much as a third of a mile long.) At its head stand three inscriptions in the Norman-French of the fourteenth century, which is still used today by the Clerks: 'Soit baillé aux Seigneurs', to send the bill from the Lower to the Upper House; 'A ceste bille les Seigneurs sont assentus', to record the Lords' agreement; and 'La Royne le veult', the formula of Royal Assent which had already been spoken in the Lords by the Clerk of the Parliaments, on behalf of Queen Elizabeth I.

THE SEVENTEENTH CENTURY

Although separate Parliamentary papers, such as Letters and Petitions, survive in quantity from the reign of James I, yet the Journals of the two Houses continue to tell the main story of Parliament. One of the most dramatic entries is that in the Commons' Journal (Plate 3, page 7), of the discovery of the Gunpowder Plot to blow up King, Lords and Commons at the opening of a new session in 1605. The Clerk has squeezed his record of this into the margin, opposite a routine entry concerning members appointed to a Committee. *[continued on page 8]*

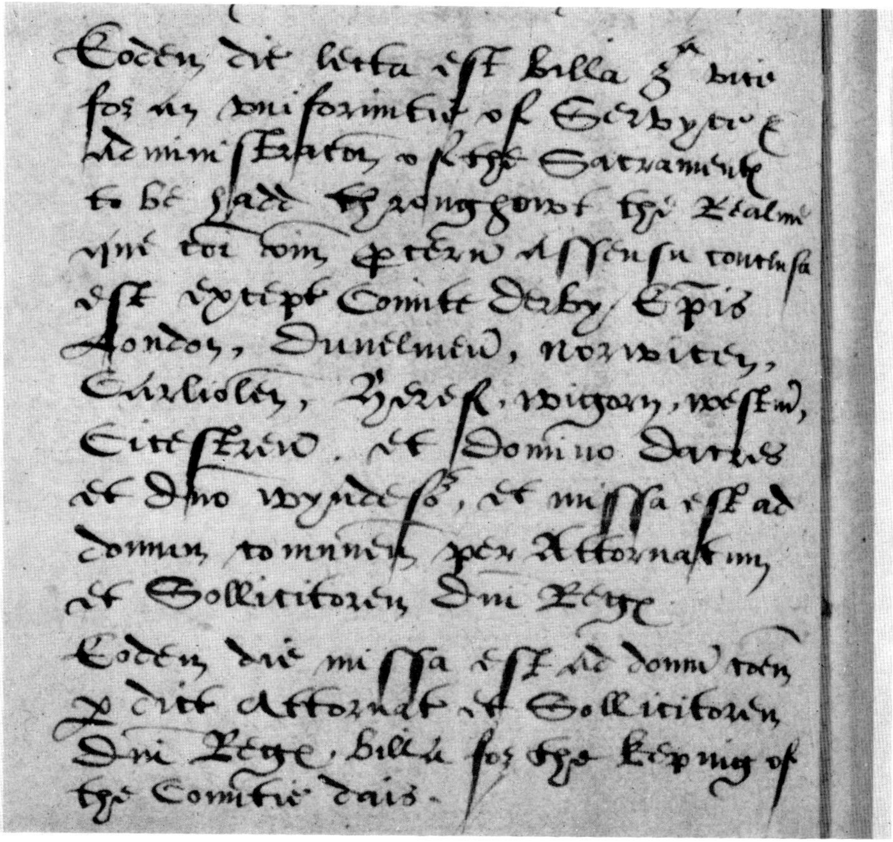

PLATE I (see page 4). *The Lords' Journal Recording the Passing of the First Act of Uniformity, 15th January 1549*

The text reads: '*Eodem die lecta est billa 3a vice* [The same day the bill was read a third time] for an uniformitie of Servyce & / administrac[i]on of the Sacramentes / to be hadd throughowt the Realme / *que co[mmun]i om[nium] proceru[m] assensu conclusa / est except[is] Comite Derby Ep[isop]is / London, Dunelmen', Norwicen, / Carliolen', Heref', Wigorn, Westm', / Cicestren', et Domino Dacres / et D[omi]no Wyndesor, et missa est ad / domum com[m]unem per Attornatum / et Sollicitorem D[omi]ni Regis. / . . .* [which was concluded by common assent of all peers, excepting the Earl of Derby, the Bishops of London, Durham, Norwich, Carlisle, Hereford, Worcester, Westminster, Chichester and Lord Dacres and Lord Windsor, and was sent to the Commons House by the Attorney and Solicitor of the Lord King . . .]'. The list of peers present shows that 2 archbishops, 18 bishops, and 31 temporal lords, as well as Protector Somerset, were in the House.

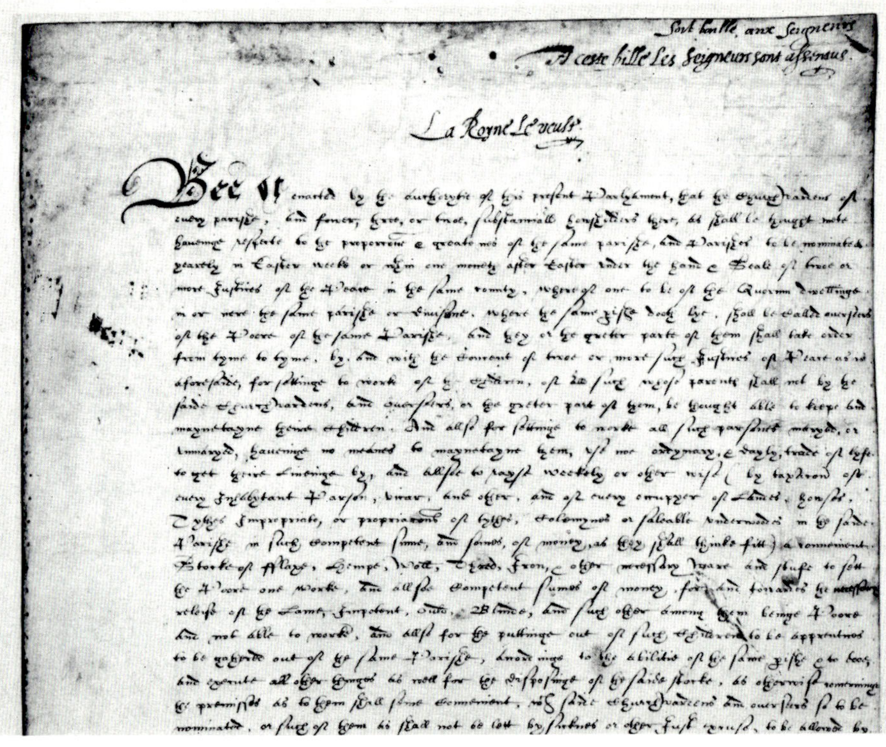

PLATE 2. *An Original Act: The Poor Law of 1601 (43 Eliz. I, no. 2)*

At the head of the roll are the Norman-French formulae, mentioned on page 4. They may be translated as: 'Let it be delivered to the Lords'; 'To this bill the Lords have agreed'; 'The Queen wills it'. The text of the Act opens as follows: '*Bee yt* enacted by the aucthorytie of this present Parlyament, that the Church Wardens of / every parishe, and fower, three, or twoe, substanciall howsholders there, as shall be thought mete / haveinge respecte to the proporc[i]one & greatenes of the same parishe, and Parishes to be nominated / yearely in Easter weeke or w[i]thin one moneth after Easter under the hand & Seale of twoe or / more Justices of the Peace in the same county, whereof one to be of the Quorum dwellinge / in or nere the same parishe or divisione, where the same parishe dooth Lye, shall be Called overseers / of the Poore of the same Parishe, and they or the greter parte of them shall take order / from tyme or tyme, by and with the Concent of twoe or more such Justices of Peace as is / aforesaide, for settinge to worke of the Children, of all such whose parentes shall not by the / saide Church Wardens, and Overseers, or the greter part of them, be thought able to keepe and / maynetayne theire Children . . .' The marks down the side from which the lines were drawn for writing can be seen, as well as some of the lines themselves. The left hand margin was stained with ink when the roll was written.

6

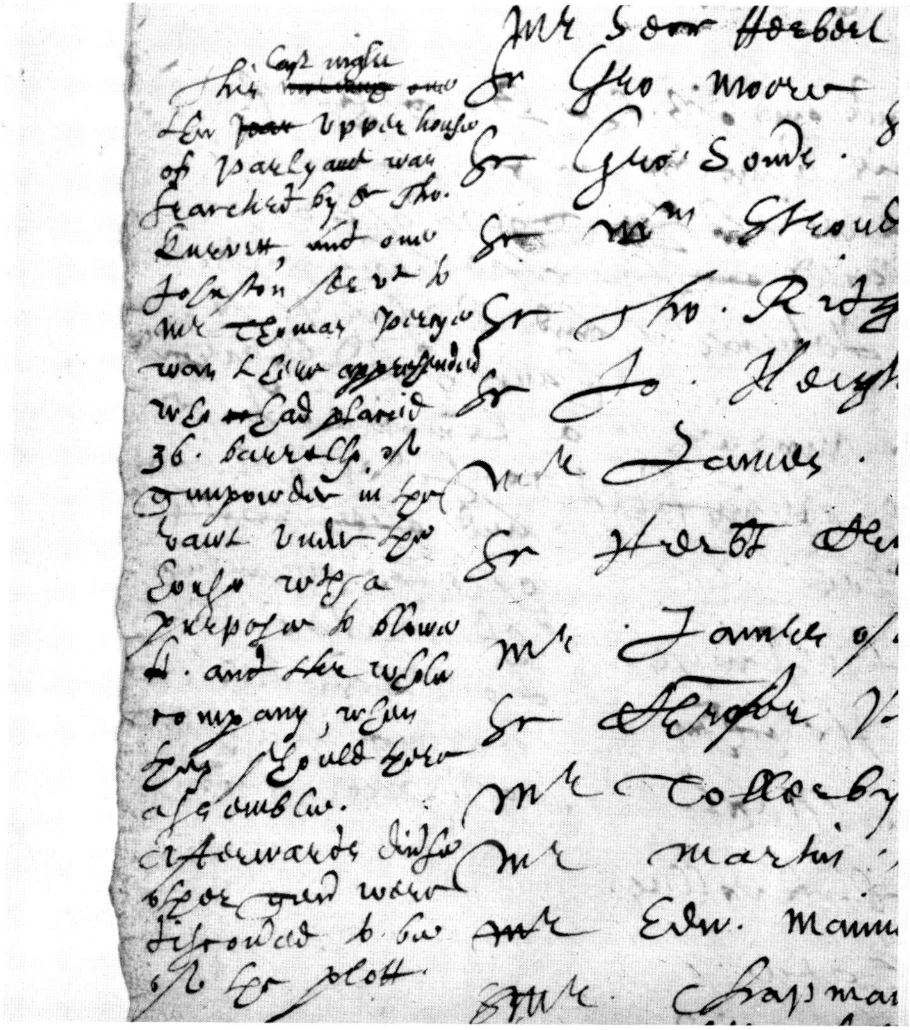

PLATE 3. *The Commons' Journal: The Gunpowder Plot, 5th November 1605*

The Clerk's note reads: 'This last night / the upper house / of Parlyam[en]t was / searched by S[i]r Tho. / Knevett, and one / Johnston serv[an]t to / Mr Thomas Percye / was there apprehended / who had placed / 36. barrelles of / gunpowder in the / Vawt under the / house w[i]th a / purpose to blowe / K. [the King] and the whole / company, when / they should there / assemble. / Afterwards div[er]se / other gen[tlemen] were / discov[er]ed to be / of the plott'.

7

PLATE 4. *The Earl of Banbury's Patent of Nobility, 18th August 1627*

The Patent is brilliantly decorated with red, blue, gold and other colours. The fine portrait of
Charles I is framed in the initial C of 'Carolus' (Charles).

[*continued from page 4*] The conflict that developed in the following generation between
King and Parliament was over small as well as great things. The Patent shown above
granted Viscount Wallingford the Earldom of Banbury and also a remarkable prece-
dence over all other earls created since 1625. It started a dispute between Lords and
King concerning this peerage that lasted until after the Restoration, and led in 1661
to the Patent being laid before the House—which then added it to its archives.

Conflict on more fundamental points led to Charles I being forced to assent to the 'Petition of Right' in 1628 by which royal authority was curtailed in four directions: billeting of soldiers, martial law, taxation and imprisonment. It was in fact a Bill, but the royal reply was given on 2nd June 1628 with a long and unusual formula reciting that 'The King willeth, That Right be done, according to the Laws and Customs of the Realm. And that the Statutes be put in due Execution, that His Subjects may have no Cause to complain of any Wrongs or Oppressions contrary to their just Rights and Liberties; to the Preservation whereof he holds Himself in Conscience as well obliged as of his Prerogative.' This answer both Lords and Commons considered not 'clear and satisfactory', and eventually the King attended the House on 7th June 1628 and commanded 'the said Clerk to cut off His former Answer, which was written

PLATE 5(a). *The Petition of Right, 1628*

showing the writing loops of the original Royal Reply remaining at the foot of the parchment

under the said Petition, and to write down His Answer which he now delivered unto the same'. This was a formula of assent, 'Soit droit fait come est desiré', which had the effect of making the petition an Act of Parliament.

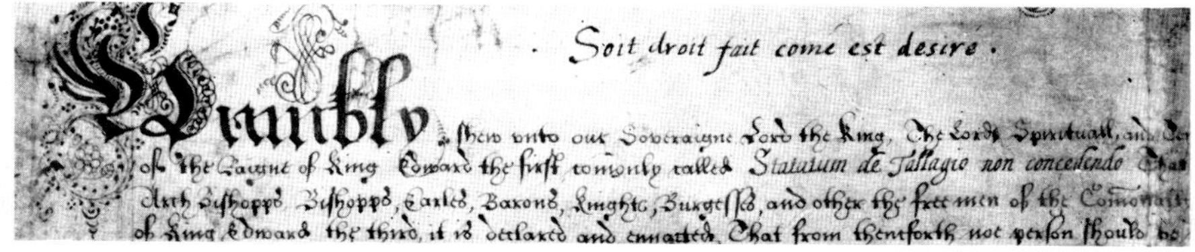

PLATE 5(b). *The Petition of Right, 1628*

showing the formula of Royal Assent, 'Soit droit fait come est desire' ('let right be done as is desired')

Very many papers survive to document the last stage in the struggle between King and Parliament, from 1640 until 1649, of which perhaps the most poignant is that shown in Plate 6 (page 10), the letter of Charles I finally assenting to the execution of his minister, the Earl of Strafford. All substantial co-operation between King and Parliament ended with the King's attempt to arrest the five Members in 1642, of which we have the record made by the Clerk as Charles stood by the table and spoke to the House (Plate 7). [*continued on page 12*]

9

My Lords, I did yesterday satisfie the Justice of the Kingdome by the passing of the Bill of Attaindour against the Earle of Strafford: but Mercie being as inherent & inseperable to a King as Justice, I desyre, at this tyme, in some measure, to show that lykewais, by suffering that unfortunat Man to fullfill the naturall course of his lyfe, in a close Imprisonment, yet so, that if euer he make the least offer to escape, or offer, directlie or indirectlie to medle in anie sorte of publike businesse, espetiallie with mee, by eather messadge or letter, it shall coste him his lyfe, without further Processe: This, if it may bee done, without a discontentment to my People, would be an unspeacable contentment to mee: To wch end, as in the first place, I, by this letter, doe earnestlie desyre your approbation (& to endeare it the more, haue chosen him to carry it, that of all your Howse, is most cleare to me) so I desyre that by a conference, ye would endeauor to giue the Howse of Comons, contentment lykewais: asseuring you, that the exercising of Mercy is no more pleasing to me, then to see bothe my Howses of Parlaments content for my sake, that I should moderat the severitie of a Law, in so important a Case: I will not say, that your complying with mee, in this my intended Mercie shall make me more willing, but certainelie, it will make me more cheerfull in granting your just Grevances: but if no lesse then his lyfe, cann satisfie my People, I must say Fiat Justitia: Thus againe earnestlie recomending the consideration of my soveraigntye unto you, I rest

If he must Dey, it wer a Charitie to repryue until Saterday

Your unalterable affectionat frend
Charles R

Whythall the 11 of May 1641

PLATE 6. *King Charles I's Letter Assenting to the Execution of the Earl of Strafford, 11th May 1641*

This is written in the King's own hand and shows various alterations made by him.

10

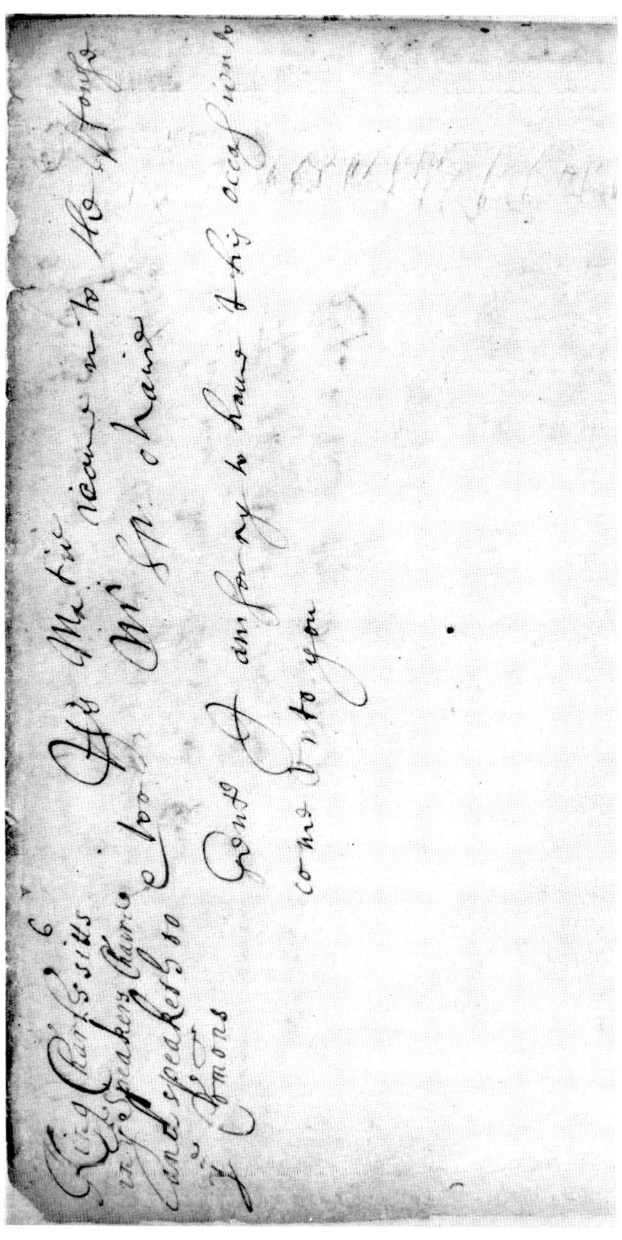

PLATE 7. *Commons' Journal: Attempted Arrest of the Five Members, 4th January 1642*

The Clerk has written: 'His Ma[jes]tie (i)came into the House
& took Mr Sp[eaker's] chaire
Gent[lemen] I am sorry to have this occasion [to]
come unto you'

Here the entry breaks off as the King went on to ask Mr. Speaker Lenthall where the missing members were. The Speaker replied 'I have neither eyes to see, nor tongue to speak in this place, but as this House is pleased to direct me'. The King seeing the five members had hurriedly left, said 'I see all the birds are flown'. As he walked out, members cried 'Privilege, privilege' after him. A later Clerk wrote the side heading 'King Charles sitts in ye Speakers Chaire and speaketh to ye Co[m]ons'.

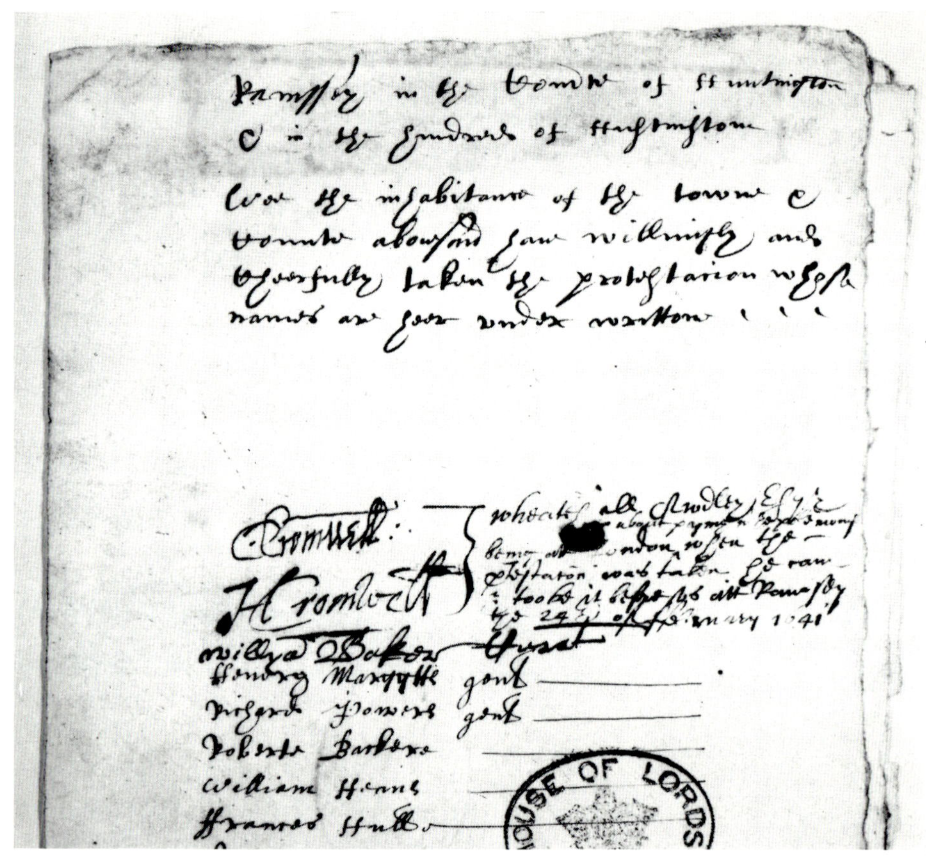

PLATE 8. *Cromwell's uncle and cousin witness a Protestation, 24th February 1642*

[*continued from page 9*] The attempt to arrest the five Members, amongst other results, led the Commons to order all men over eighteen to take a Protestation 'against all Popery and Popish Innovations'. The resulting 'Protestation Returns', which now survive amongst the Lords' records, are very frequently consulted today by those tracing their family history and by those concerned with the statistics of population. The return shown in Plate 8 (above) is from Ramsey in Huntingdonshire. At its head Sir Oliver and Henry Cromwell sign their names above that of the Curate of the parish. They witness that 'Wheatehill Awdley Esqr / being att London about paying in the pole mony when the / protestac[i]on was taken he cam / & tooke it before us att Ramsey / the 24th of February 1641[/2]'. The course of the Civil War that

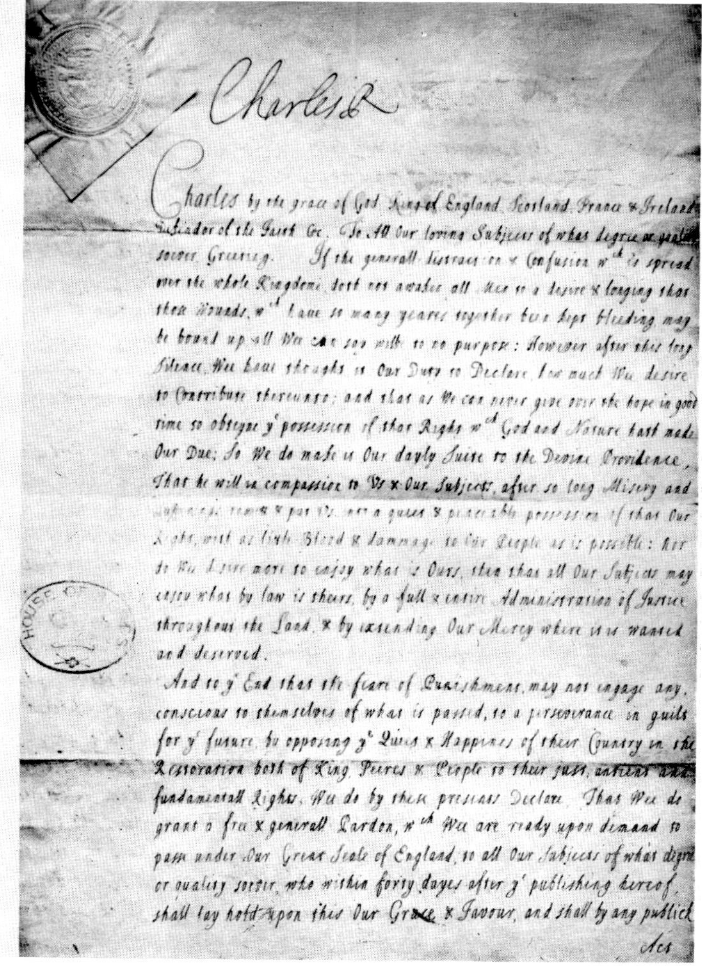

PLATE 9. *The Declaration of Breda, 4th April 1660*

followed is represented by many documents at the House of Lords, not least by the famous 'Naseby Letters' left behind by Charles I on the battlefield of Naseby. The final outcome was the return of his son in 1660 and the Restoration Settlement, based on the 'Declaration of Breda' sent by Charles II from Holland to Parliament and shown above. By it Charles promised an almost entire pardon to his enemies, payment of arrears of wages to the Ironside army; a settlement of the land question; and religious liberty. The compromise of 1660 proved unworkable, and the 'Glorious Revolution' in

That the raiseing or keeping of a standing Army
within the Kingdome in time of peace unlesse it
bee with consent of Parliament is against Law
That the subjects which are Protestants may
~~provide and keep~~ Armes for their ~~common~~ defence
~~suitable to their condicion as allowed by Law~~
That election of Members of Parliament ought
to bee free.
That the freedome of Speech and debates or
proceedings in Parliament ought not to bee
impeached or questioned in any Court or place
out of Parliament.
That excessive Bayle ought not to be required
nor excessive ffynes imposed nor cruell and unusu-
all Punishments inflicted.
That Jurors ought to be duely impannelled
and returned and Jurors which passe upon men
in tryalls for high treason ought to bee freeholders
That all Grants and promises of ffynes and
forfeitures of perticuler persons before convic-
tion are illegall and void.

PLATE 10. *The Declaration of Rights, 12th February 1689*

1688–9 established a new régime setting more precise limits to royal authority. This
was expressed in the Parliamentary Declaration, part of which, as amended by the
Lords, is shown above. The Deputy Clerk of the Parliaments read this Declaration to
the Prince and Princess of Orange on 13th February and they, accepting its terms,
became King and Queen as William III and Mary II. The Declaration was later incor-
porated into the well-known 'Bill of Rights' to become perhaps the fundamental
constitutional document of the modern period. The new order was completed by the
union of the two kingdoms of England and Scotland in 1707 (see Plate 11 opposite).
[*continued on page 16*]

PLATE II. *The Articles of Union between England and Scotland*

showing the first pages of signatures appended on 22nd July 1706 by the English Commissioners (in the left-hand columns) and the Scottish (in the right-hand). The Act ratifying the Articles was passed in 1707 (6 Anne c.11)

PAPERS OF RECENT CENTURIES

The volume of papers laid on the Table of the House increases greatly in the eighteenth and nineteenth centuries, and only three examples can be given here, two of which relate to political history, the third to economic. Below (Plate 12 (a)) is the conclusion of a despairing petition written by Warren Hastings to the House in the sixth year of his long-drawn out impeachment before it. Beneath that (Plate 12 (b)) is part of the Test Roll signed by Lord Nelson on 29th October 1801. He had clearly been told to delete his Italian title of [Duke of] Bronté. On page 17 (Plate 13) is a single example of the many thousands of plans and other documents deposited with the two Houses in connection with the construction of canals, railways and other public works, which constitute a principal source for the study of the Industrial Revolution.

[continued on page 19]

PLATE 12(a). *Petition of Warren Hastings, 18th April 1793*

PLATE 12(b). *The Test (or Oath) Roll of 1801*

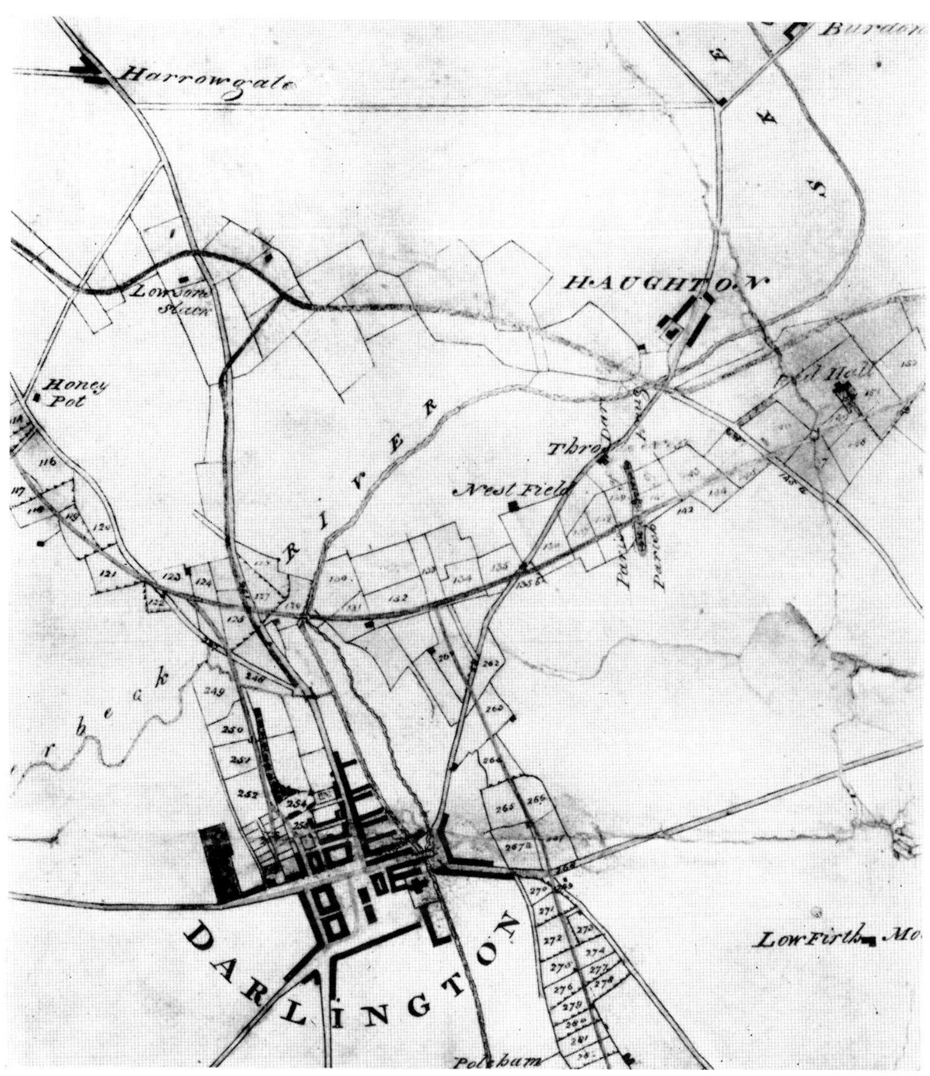

PLATE 13. *The Plan signed by George Stephenson for the Stockton & Darlington Railway (Deviation) Bill, 1823*

This shows the part relating to the village of Darlington. The original line is near Haughton; the proposed new line and the branch to Darlington are shown running through a series of numbered pieces of property. This property is described in an annexed 'Book of Reference'

17

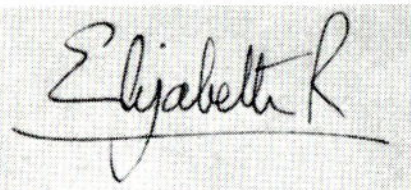

Elizabeth the Second by the Grace of God of the United Kingdom of Great Britain and Northern Ireland and of Our other Realms and Territories Queen Head of the Commonwealth Defender of the Faith TO Our right trusty and right well beloved the Lords Spiritual and Temporal and to Our trusty and well beloved the Knights Citizens and Burgesses of the House of Commons in this present Parliament assembled GREETING:

FORASMUCH as in Our said Parliament divers Acts have been agreed upon by you Our loving subjects the Lords Spiritual and Temporal and the Commons the short Titles of which are set forth in the Schedule hereto but the said Acts are not of force and effect in the Law without Our Royal Assent AND forasmuch as We cannot at this time be present in the Higher House of Our said Parliament being the accustomed place for giving Our Royal Assent to such Acts as have been agreed upon by you Our said subjects the Lords and Commons WE have therefore caused these Our Letters Patent to be made and have signed them and by them do give Our Royal Assent to the said Acts WILLING that the said Acts shall be of the same strength force and effect as if We had been personally present in the said Higher House and had publicly and in the presence of you all assented to the same COMMANDING ALSO Our most dear Cousin and Counsellor David Viscount Kilmuir

Chancellor of Great Britain to seal these Our Letters Patent with Our Great Seal of Our Realm AND ALSO COMMANDING Our most dear and entirely beloved Uncle and most faithful Counsellor Henry William Frederick Albert DUKE OF GLOUCESTER—The Most Reverend Father in God and Our faithful Counsellor Geoffrey Francis ARCHBISHOP OF CANTERBURY Primate of All England and Metropolitan —Our most dear Cousin and Counsellor David Viscount Kilmuir

Chancellor of Great Britain— Our well beloved and faithful Counsellors Harold Harington Lord Balfour of Inchrye - Francis Aungier Lord Pakenham -

or any three or more of them to declare this Our Royal Assent in the said Higher House in the presence of you the said Lords and Commons and the Clerk of Our Parliaments to endorse the said Acts in Our name as is requisite and to enrol these Our Letters Patent and the said Acts in manner accustomed AND FINALLY

PLATE 14. *Commission, signed by H.M. The Queen, for giving Royal Assent to the Rating and Valuation Act of 1959 and 13 other Acts, 14th May 1959*

The pencil marks were made by the then Reading Clerk to guide him in reading the document aloud in the House. The Great Seal impressed on the second page of the document shows through in reverse

CONTEMPORARY RECORDS

Nowadays, in the summer of each year, the records of the previous year's session are assembled from the various departments of the two Houses, for deposit in the Victoria Tower. Some 3,000 separate documents accumulate, on the average, from each year's work, and, amongst them, are representatives of most of the classes of record already described: acts, plans, Journals, petitions, and, most numerous of all, the papers laid on the Table of the House, which today range from reports of Royal Commissions to statistics and other papers submitted by Government departments. In recent years the records have been further enriched by the deposit of the parliamentary and political papers of members of both Houses, outstanding amongst which is the collection of papers of Sir Herbert Samuel, 1st Viscount Samuel.

As a final example of the records of Parliament, a document has been chosen (Plate 14) which itself marks the final stage in the principal work of Parliament, the enacting of laws. It is the Letters Patent under the Great Seal by which Her Majesty instructed three or more of five peers (who are named), to declare her Royal Assent to 14 bills which had passed through both Houses of Parliament. This method of giving the Royal Assent was first used on 11th February 1542, for the remarkable purpose of sparing King Henry VIII from having to attend in person to assent to the Bill for the attainder of Queen Katharine Howard. The device of assenting by a Royal Commission was thereafter employed frequently, and between 1854 and 1967, every Act of Parliament was passed in this way. The scene at the most famous Royal Assent by Commission of all time, that by which the Reform Bill of 1832 became law, is depicted in the illustration on page iii of the cover.

The Letters Patent of 1959 thus afford yet one more example of the way in which the records of Parliament may enshrine within themselves both an account of contemporary events, and also, in so many instances, much of the history and procedure of past centuries. The contents of the Victoria Tower thus form the constantly expanding historic memory of Parliament, and, as such, are a significant part of the heritage of Britain, and also of those many lands overseas which today share in her constitutional and cultural tradition.

HOUSE OF LORDS RECORD OFFICE The documents illustrated in this booklet are preserved in the Victoria Tower at the Houses of Parliament in the care of the House of Lords Record Office. The Search Room of that office is open throughout the year to all members of the public who wish to study specific documents. Preliminary enquiries should be made in writing to the Clerk of the Records, House of Lords Record Office, London SW1A 0PW.

PUBLICATION OF PARLIAMENTARY DOCUMENTS Her Majesty's Stationery Office publish a series of reproductions of documents belonging to the records of both Houses and also a series of volumes of Calendars of the Lords Manuscripts. Lists of the reproductions and of the volumes of the Calendar available may be obtained from the Clerk of the Records at the House of Lords.

The picture opposite illustrates the most famous of all Assents by Commission—the last stage in the progress of the Reform Bill of 1832. The Tory benches were empty as the deputy Clerk of the Parliaments turned towards the Commons to pronounce the formula, 'Le Roy le veult'. The Bill itself is unrolled on the table beside him, covering the dispatch box and falling to the ground. The chief Commissioner, in a black three-cornered hat, is Lord Brougham, the Lord Chancellor.

ACKNOWLEDGEMENTS

The illustration reproduced on page ii of the cover appears by gracious permission of Her Majesty The Queen; the original is preserved in the Royal Library at Windsor Castle. The remaining illustrations have been prepared by the Reproductions Branch of the Air Ministry Photographic Section, excepting the photograph on page 3, which is reproduced with acknowledgements to A. F. Kersting. Her Majesty's Stationery Office is responsible for the typographic design.

Printed in England for Her Majesty's Stationery Office
by Ebenezer Baylis and Son Limited, The Trinity Press, Worcester, and London

Dd 288290 K30 2/75